Outlaws and Lawmen of the Wild West

WYATT EARP

Carl R. Green
⇾ and ⇽
William R. Sanford

ENSLOW PUBLISHERS, INC.
Bloy St. & Ramsey Ave.   P.O. Box 38
Box 777   Aldershot
Hillside, N.J. 07205   Hants GU12 6BP
U.S.A.   U.K.

Library of Congress Cataloging-in-Publication Data

Green, Carl R.
    Wyatt Earp / Carl R. Green and William R. Sanford.
        p. cm. — (Outlaws and lawmen of the wild west)
    Includes bibliographical references and index.
    Summary: Chronicles the life of the Western lawman Wyatt Earp.
    ISBN 0-89490-367-5
    1. Earp, Wyatt, 1848–1929—Juvenile literature. 2. Peace officers—Southwest,
New—Biography—Juvenile literature. 3. Tombstone (Ariz.)—History—Juvenile lit-
erature. [1. Earp, Wyatt, 1848–1929. 2. Peace officers.] I. Sanford, William R. (William
Reynolds), 1927– . II. Title. III. Series: Green, Carl R. Outlaws and lawmen of the
wild west.
F786.E18674 1992
978.02′092—dc20
[B]   91-29855
                                                                    CIP
                                                                     AC

Printed in the United States of America

10 9 8 7 6 5 4 3 2

Illustration Credits:
Amon Carter Museum, Fort Worth, Texas, p. 17; Arizona Historical Society Library,
pp. 9, 12, 18, 22, 24, 25, 26, 30, 32, 38; Denver Public Library, Western History
Department, pp. 6, 41; Carl R. Green and William R. Sanford, pp. 11, 33; Mullin
Collection, N.S. Haley Memorial Library, pp. 29, 36, 39, 43.

Cover Illustration:
Michael David Biegel

CONTENTS

AUTHORS' NOTE

This book tells the true story of a lawman named Wyatt Earp. Wyatt was as well known a hundred years ago as rocks stars are now. His exploits appeared in newspapers, magazines, and dime novels. In more recent times Wyatt has been featured in movies and a television series. Some of the stories were made up, but many were true. The events described in this book all come from first hand reports.

1

THE BUNTLINE SPECIAL

In 1876 Dodge City, Kansas was called the toughest town on the prairies. Cowboys who drove their cattle there from Texas stayed to drink, play cards, and fight. The trouble grew worse after the deputy marshal was driven out of town. Slow-moving, 300-pound Marshal Deger could not keep the peace. To save Dodge, the town council sent for Wyatt Earp.

Wyatt was a good choice for the job. He soon tamed Dodge's wild nightlife. Cowboys out for a spree backed down under Wyatt's icy stare. The young marshal's success in Dodge added to his growing fame.

A few weeks later, legend tells us, Ned Buntline came to town. Buntline wrote for the popular magazines known as dime novels. He said he had come to Dodge to honor the lawmen he featured in his tales. To Wyatt and four others, he gave special Colt six-guns. These

One hard look from the steely blue eyes of Wyatt Earp could quell a riot or disarm a rowdy cowboy. Ned Buntline, a well-known writer, wrote about Wyatt's work in the Kansas cowtowns. Buntline gave Wyatt a special Colt pistol as a tribute to his skill as a lawman.

Buntline Specials had twelve-inch barrels—four inches longer than most Colts. The guns also had carved handles and fine holsters.

Wyatt carried the long-barreled gun on his right hip. The extra length did not slow down his fast draw. Yet Wyatt was not quick on the trigger. Even when he had a gun in his hand, he seldom shot anyone. One night he found two cowboys behind a dance hall. One of them fired at him, but missed. Instead of shooting back Wyatt smashed the heavy gun against the cowboy's head. The man fell to the ground, knocked out cold.

Cool action was Wyatt's style. He said that hitting a man over the head was better than shooting him. If asked, the cowboy would surely have agreed. Waking up with a headache was better than not waking up at all!

2
GROWING UP
TO BE A LAWMAN

Wyatt Berry Stapp Earp was born in Monmouth, Illinois on March 19, 1848. He was the fifth of eight children. His parents, Nicholas and Virginia Earp, were from Kentucky. Nicholas was trained as a lawyer, but farming was his first love. He also had a high sense of duty. After moving to Illinois, Nicholas served as an unpaid lawman. Then, with the outbreak of the Mexican War he joined the U.S. Army as a captain. Wyatt was named for the man who led his father's unit during the war.

When Wyatt was two years old the family moved to Pella, Iowa. This was frontier country. At times the only law was that of the six-gun. Nicholas thought it was the duty of good men to stand up for what was right. He drummed that message into the heads of his children. He also valued learning. When they outgrew the village schools, the Earp children studied at home. They also learned to stick together—in good times and bad.

From Iowa Nicholas hoped to move to California. The death of Martha, Wyatt's older sister, delayed the move. Then, in 1861, came the Civil War. Nicholas and the three older boys—Newton, James, and Virgil—joined the Union army. Young Wyatt had to stay home. With the help of his brothers Morgan and Warren, he raised eighty acres of corn. However, because army life sounded more exciting, Wyatt ran away to enlist. To his

Virgil Earp (right) was the oldest of the gunslinging Earp brothers. Hot-tempered Morgan Earp (left) was one of Wyatt's two younger brothers. As a lawman he gained renown as a "town tamer" in Dodge City, Kansas and Butte, Montana.

surprise the first soldier he met was his father! Nicholas sent his young son back to the cornfields.

In 1864 Nicholas left the army. He bought two covered wagons and set out for the West Coast. Other families from Pella and Monmouth joined Earp's wagon train. Wyatt, strong for his age, drove one of the wagons. It was an adult's job, but he did it well. Hunting was Wyatt's second job. Thanks to his skill there was fresh meat for each night's meal.

The difficult trip took seven months. After crossing the Mojave Desert the Earps settled in San Bernardino. Nicholas bought a ranch and later served as a county judge. He expected Wyatt to study law, but the boy did not listen.

Young Wyatt ran off and found work as a stagecoach driver. One of his stage runs was from San Bernardino to Los Angeles. Another took him across the desert to Prescott, Arizona. In 1868 he went to Wyoming to help build the Union Pacific Railroad. Wyatt soon showed he could handle the mule teams used to grade the roadbed. He also revealed a sharp head for business. After saving some money, he bought his own mule teams and hired men to drive them. When the job was done, he had saved up $2,500.

In 1870 Wyatt went back to Illinois. While he was there he wed Urilla Sutherland. Sadly, the marriage ended that same year when Urilla died of typhus. From there Wyatt joined a party that was mapping the Indian

Territory in what is now Oklahoma. Hired as a hunter, he carried two pistols, a rifle, and a shotgun.

After this job was done Wyatt spent the summer of 1871 in Kansas City. He was young and had money in his pocket. Much of his cash went for whiskey, cards, and dance hall girls. Some reports say that he got mixed up in horse stealing. Free on a $500 bond, he fled before his case came to trial.

Kansas was wide-open in the years after the Civil War. Cowboys drove cattle north from Texas to meet the newly-built railroads. Then, with money in their jeans, they went looking for a good time. They drank, gambled, and settled fights with fists and six-guns. Lawmen

The coming of the railroad changed sleepy Kansas towns into rip-roaring cowtowns. Wyatt Earp made his name as a lawman by taming the cowboys of Wichita and Dodge City.

tried—often in vain—to keep the peace. Arresting armed, drunken cowboys took courage. As it turned out Wyatt Earp had that type of nerve.

Wyatt now stood 6 feet 2 inches tall and weighed 185 pounds. Women liked his blue eyes, straight nose, and drooping mustache. When he was angry those blue eyes turned steely and cold. Like most men, he was neither all good nor all bad. Even his critics agreed that he was brave and loyal. He did not look for fights, but neither did he back down from them.

In 1873 Wyatt drifted into Ellsworth, Kansas. Cattle grazed the lush grass outside of town. Tough cowboys filled the saloons. Like most cowtowns, it was a violent place.

Wyatt Earp stands high on any list of the best lawmen of the Wild West. In an era well known for shootouts and killing, he seldom shot anyone. He faced drunken cowboys and lynch mobs with a cool courage that often calmed tempers and saved lives. When cowtowns needed a strong lawman, Wyatt was the man for the job.

When they were working cattle, cowboys put in long, hard days. Once the work was done, they wanted to relax. For most of them, that meant whiskey, cards, and fighting. Riding herd on a town full of fun-loving cowboys was a tough job for a lawman.

One day Wyatt saw a gambler named Bill Thompson shoot the sheriff. As Bill fled, his brother Ben covered his escape with a shotgun. Ben was backed up by at least one hundred Texans. The town's police force looked at the well-armed cowboys and turned away. Mayor Miller fired his gun-shy lawmen. Then he gave Wyatt a badge. "I order you to arrest Ben Thompson," the mayor said.

Wyatt knew what his father would have done. He buckled on a pair of six-guns and walked out on the dusty street. Ben watched him, shotgun in hand. As Wyatt came closer he kept his eyes on Ben's hands. If those hands moved he was ready to draw and fire. When Wyatt reached a point fifteen yards away Ben asked him what he wanted. Wyatt said he was there to arrest Ben— or to kill him. Ben must have sensed that Wyatt meant what he said. He threw down his shotgun and raised his hands.

His first day as a lawman in Ellsworth was also Wyatt's last. A judge fined Ben Thompson only $25 and told Wyatt to give him back his guns. The small fine told Wyatt that the town would not stand behind him. He turned in his badge and left.

Ben Thompson was well known as a gambler and a gunslinger. Word that a young lawman had faced him down spread quickly. Wyatt now had a reputation. Any town needing a marshal would have been glad to hire him.

3

CLEANING UP THE COWTOWNS

In 1874 cowboys were running wild in Wichita, Kansas. When Wyatt came to town the mayor tried to hire him as deputy marshal. Wyatt did not need the job, but it was clear the town needed him. After the mayor promised to back him, Wyatt pinned on the badge. The city gave him two Colt forty-fives and $125 a month. The good pay pleased Wyatt. Most lawmen were paid far less.

Wyatt did not waste any time. He went around town hiding shotguns in stores and saloons. The weapons would come in handy if anyone tried to run him out. Some Texas cowboys hated Wyatt for what he had done to Ben Thompson.

Abel "Shanghai" Pierce, a rich Texas cattle king, was staying in town. Like the men who worked for him, Shanghai liked to drink. One day Wyatt found him yelling drunken oaths on the main street. He took Shanghai's gun away and told him to lay off the whiskey.

A few hours later some Texans carried Shanghai out to the street. They shouted threats and fired their guns in the air. The shooting alarmed the men of Wichita, who had their guns ready. Bloodshed was in the air.

Wyatt had to act fast. He grabbed a shotgun, ran down an alley, and circled behind the cowboys. Wyatt's quick move took the mob by surprise. Pointing the shotgun at their leader, he told the cowboys to put up their hands. The leader looked at the shotgun and dropped his six-gun. Shanghai woke up long enough to tell the others to do the same. Wyatt then marched the Texans to the courthouse. As a judge found each man guilty, Shanghai paid the $100 fines.

The cowboys were boiling mad and vowed to get even. They picked Mannen Clements to lead them. Clements was known to be a killer. For his part Wyatt rounded up a posse to defend the town. When told the Texans were coming he lined his men up on the main street. Soon he saw forty cowboys crossing the bridge into town. Wyatt met the Texans there.

Clements was holding a gun in each hand. He looked at the marshal. Wyatt's hands were swinging free, close to his twin six-guns. He told Clements to go back to his camp. The two men stared at each other. Clements blinked first. Slowly he put his guns away. As Wyatt watched, still on guard, the cowboys went back across

16

As a Dodge City lawman, Wyatt tracked down horse thieves and cattle rustlers. When he was on the trail, Wyatt dressed like a typical cowboy. In town, he wore white shirts, string ties, and long black coats.

the bridge. That was the last time they tried to shoot up the main street. Within two years the violence had moved westward to Dodge City.

In the spring of 1876 Dodge City badly needed a strong lawman. Some people were calling it the most wicked cowtown in the West. The saloons were filled with cowboys, buffalo hunters, and railroad workers. Gamblers and thieves raked in the easy money. Gunfights were a nightly event.

Mayor George Hoover sent for Wyatt. As marshal, Wyatt hired his brother Morgan to be his deputy. He also hired Bat Masterson and Bat's brother, Jim. Then he drew a line at the tracks that cut the town in half. Only

Bat Masterson served as one of Wyatt Earp's deputies in Dodge City. Bat dressed like a city slicker, but he was a fine lawman. Like Wyatt, Bat would rather "buffalo" a rowdy cowboy than shoot him. As Wyatt explained it, "to buffalo" meant "bending a six-gun over a man's head."

lawmen were allowed to carry guns north of that line. Cowboys and farmers had to check their guns at racks kept in hotels, stores, and saloons. Wyatt and his deputies used their own guns only as a last resort. Bat patrolled Front Street with a walking stick in his hand. Sometimes he used it to club drunken hoodlums.

This Dodge City police force made ten or more arrests a day. Some men went to jail with heads bloodied by Wyatt's Buntline Special. But Wyatt also fought with his fists. In one fight a cowboy tried to rake Wyatt with his spurs. The marshal quickly stepped aside and hit the man in the stomach. A crowd pressed in to watch. Before the cowboy knew what was happening, Wyatt's second blow ended the fight. The marshal's shirt was still a spotless white.

When the cattle drives ended that fall, Wyatt looked over his record. He had kept the peace in Dodge City for eight months. During that time dozens of men spent time in the city jail. The deputies had collected thousands of dollars in fines. As was often the custom, the lawmen split the fines.

As for shootings, only two men had been killed. That compared to over seventy in the four years before Wyatt came to Dodge. Thanks to his cool leadership, the police had not killed anyone. Wyatt was credited with taming the rowdy cowtown.

With the cowboys back in Texas, Dodge City became quiet. Restless as always, Wyatt yearned to prospect for

Dodge City was quiet during the months between cattle drives. That gave Wyatt and Morgan time to prospect for gold in the Black Hills. By the time they reached Deadwood, however, all the good claims were taken. Morgan left, but Wyatt stayed on.

gold. With Morgan beside him he headed north to the Dakotas.

Deadwood City was the center of the Black Hills gold strike. However, Wyatt soon learned that all the good claims had been taken. To make things worse the first snows were already falling. Morgan hurried back to Dodge, but Wyatt stayed in Deadwood. He was one of the few men who still had their horses with them. If he could not strike gold, Wyatt thought, he could at least "mine the miners."

Firewood was in short supply. To help solve the problem, Wyatt rigged up a wagon box that could be pulled on runners or on wheels. Then he bought wood for $2 a cord. The miners paid him $12 a cord to haul it to Deadwood. One man paid $100 for a night delivery— he needed the wood to keep a poker game going. By the time spring came Wyatt had $5,000 in his pocket.

When Wyatt left Deadwood, Wells Fargo hired him to guard the Cheyenne stagecoach. A guard was needed because the stage carried a fortune in gold. Wyatt, riding shotgun, took his place next to the driver. Along the way, two outlaw bands chased the stage. Wyatt calmly opened fire, driving them away.

Wyatt stayed on guard for the full 300-mile trip. Even though he had saved the gold, Wells Fargo paid him only $50. But Wyatt never lacked a job for long. In Cheyenne a telegram was waiting. Would Wyatt go back to Dodge City? The cowboys were tearing up the town again.

4
THE EARPS MOVE TO TOMBSTONE

Wyatt cracked down hard on the Texas cowboys. As before he kept a tight rein on their high spirits. Each cowboy he arrested had to pay a fine of $2.50. In the first month Wyatt collected nearly $1,000. He called it "taming the cowboys." Virgil and Morgan Earp worked as Wyatt's deputies.

Wyatt's strict rules annoyed the cowboys. So did his friendship with hot-tempered Doc Holliday. Doc was a part-time dentist and full-time gambler. Although he had a lung disease, Doc was still a crack shot. He was a good man to have at your side in a fight.

Word soon spread that Wyatt was in danger. The Texans, it was said, would pay a reward to anyone who killed the marshal. A gunslinger named Clay Allison tried, but failed. Wyatt turned the tables by driving Allison out of town. Next, in July of 1878, George Hoyt made his move from horseback. As he galloped along the main street he took some wild shots at Wyatt. One bullet punched a hole in the marshal's hat. The two men then exchanged shots. When Hoyt tried to escape, Wyatt shot him off his horse at long range.

In September Tobe Driskill and his cowboy friends raced into town on their horses. After shooting up Front Street they stopped at a saloon for a drink. As he walked into the saloon Driskill saw Wyatt standing at the bar. Before Wyatt could reach his shotgun, Driskill and his pal drew on him.

It was a tight spot. If Wyatt made a move they would

Gunslinger Doc Holliday was one of Wyatt's best friends. Doc was trained as a dentist, but he made his living as a gambler. He died "with his boots off" five years after this picture was taken.

surely shoot him. At that moment Doc Holliday burst into the saloon with a six-gun in each hand. When the gunmen turned to look at Doc, Wyatt drew his Colt. With one quick blow Wyatt knocked Driskill down. A cowboy tried to shoot the marshal, but Doc's gun roared first. The cowboy went down with a bullet in his shoulder. The others raised their hands above their heads.

Wyatt handed in his badge in the fall of 1879. "I'm tired of being a target," he said. After leaving Dodge he headed west. Virgil had told him about a silver strike in Tombstone, Arizona. The desert town was set on a rocky plateau named Goose Flats. Apache Indians roamed the nearby mountains. Like most mining towns, Tombstone lived by the law of the six-gun. It was often called "the town too tough to die."

Skilled, hard-working law officers were in demand. Wyatt signed on as deputy U.S. marshal and tax collector for Pima County. The pay was good—$500 a month—and he did not have to patrol the streets. That meant he was less likely to be used for target practice. Virgil gave up looking for silver to work as a deputy town marshal. Morgan and Jim Earp soon joined their brothers. Morgan rode shotgun for Wells Fargo and Jim worked as a bartender.

Tombstone seemed to attract outlaws. The local gang leader was N. H. "Old Man" Clanton. Clanton lived on a ranch near Tombstone with his sons Ike, Phin, and Billy. Some well-known gunmen were also on Clanton's payroll. They included Curly Bill Brocius, Frank Stilwell, Frank and Tom McLaury, and Johnny Ringo. When they were not holding up stagecoaches, the outlaws ran small ranches. They stocked them with cattle stolen in Mexico. Old Man Clanton was killed on one of those raids.

The Clanton gang soon clashed with the Earps. In October 1880 Wyatt was helping Town Marshal Fred White arrest some drunks. The lawmen found Curly Bill waving a loaded pistol. As White grabbed at the gun, it went off. A bullet slammed into White's stomach. In the next instant Wyatt knocked Curly Bill flat with his pistol. Before dying White said that the shooting was an accident. Curly Bill was fined and set free.

N. H. Clanton was better known as Old Man Clanton. From his ranch outside of Tombstone, he led a gang of rustlers and robbers. Old Man Clanton ruled his gang with an iron hand. After his death, his son Ike was often out of control.

Mules did the heavy hauling for the Tombstone mines. The highest grade ore the teams pulled to the mill was worth about $15,000 a ton. The lure of that kind of money drew men from all over the country. Many were good men, but quite a few were outlaws.

Not long afterward Pima County was split in two. A deputy U.S. marshal was appointed to enforce federal laws in the new Cochise County. A county sheriff policed the parts of the county that lay outside Tombstone's city limits. In Tombstone a town marshal was given the task of keeping the peace.

Virgil took over as town marshal. Wyatt wanted the job of county sheriff, but John Behan was named to the post. Wyatt, who was still a deputy U.S. marshal, did not trust Behan. The new sheriff had many ties to the outlaws who lived near Tombstone. He even hired some of them as deputies.

Johnny Behan took the job that Wyatt wanted—sheriff of Cochise County. Behan and Wyatt were rivals in other ways, too. Wyatt stole Behan's girlfriend. He also was scornful of Behan's ties to the Clanton gang.

Doc Holliday soon showed up, drawn by the gambling and his friendship with Wyatt. The Earps were glad to see him for there had been more trouble with the Clantons. Someone had stolen Wyatt's best horse. He found the horse, but Billy Clanton was in the saddle. Wyatt had to take his mount back at gunpoint.

In January 1881 the Earps were tested by a lynch mob. The affair began when a gambler called Johnny-Behind-the-Deuce shot a miner. After Johnny was arrested a mob formed to lynch him. Virgil and Morgan tried to hide their prisoner in a bowling alley. Wyatt, always ready to help his brothers, stood guard with his shotgun. As the mob surged forward he aimed the gun at one of the leaders. His target was Dick Gird, a mine owner who employed half of the men in the mob. Faced with that deadly shotgun Gird turned and walked away. One by one, the other miners followed him.

In March masked men fired on the Tucson stage, killing the driver. A quick-thinking guard caught the reins and drove the stage to safety. When Wyatt heard the news, he set out with a posse to chase the killers. He caught Luther King, who named some Clanton men as his partners. After King was jailed, Sheriff Behan let him escape. Behan then charged Doc Holliday with the robbery. He put Doc in jail, but had to let him go for lack of proof.

Six months later a gang robbed the Bisbee stage. A witness heard one of the robbers say, "Have we got all the sugar?" Wyatt knew that a Clanton man, Frank Stilwell, liked to use that phrase. The boot tracks at the scene also pointed to Stilwell. He was arrested in Bisbee and returned to Tombstone.

Ike Clanton and Tom McLaury posted bail for their friend. Later Tom met Morgan Earp on the street and offered to fight him. Morgan refused—for the moment. But the scene was set for a showdown.

5
GUNFIGHT AT THE O.K. CORRAL

By October 1881 the Clantons were talking loudly about killing the Earps. Wyatt and his brothers heard the talk and stayed alert. The town's leading citizens were upset. They feared that outlaws would take over the town if the Clantons won a shootout. Town Marshal Virgil Earp was told to swear in Wyatt and Morgan as deputies.

Ike Clanton acted as though he owned the town. On October 25 he spent the night in Tombstone's saloons. Doc Holliday tried to pick a fight, saying, "Get out your gun and go to work." The taunt failed. Because Ike was unarmed, Doc could not draw on him.

Ike stayed up all night playing poker. In the morning, half-drunk, he armed himself with pistols and a rifle. As he walked the streets he bragged that the shooting was about to start. Virgil caught up with Ike and put him under arrest. Ike tried to draw his six-gun, but Virgil

In 1881, Tombstone, Arizona was growing fast. The buildings of the Tombstone Mining Company lie on the edge of town. The town looks peaceful enough, but this was the year of the shootout at the O.K. Corral.

used Wyatt's trick. He knocked Ike out with one swing of his pistol.

Wyatt caught up with Ike at the courtroom and told him to behave. Ike snarled that he would take care of Wyatt later. Morgan took Ike's guns away, and the outlaw paid his $25 fine. Billy Claibourne then took his boss to have his head bandaged.

The Clantons and the McLaurys met later near the O.K. Corral. Billy Clanton told Ike he should go back to the ranch. Ike said he would go, but not just yet. In the meantime the Earps heard that the Clantons were ready to fight. Wyatt told his brothers they could no longer avoid a showdown.

Wyatt, Virgil, and Morgan set off on the long walk to the corral. The three tall men were all dressed in long black coats and black hats. Doc Holliday hurried up to join them. Wyatt told Doc that it was not his fight. That hurt Doc's feelings. Virgil stepped in, saying they would need Doc if there was shooting. He made Doc a deputy and gave him a shotgun to hide under his coat.

The lawmen turned the corner onto Fremont Street. Now they could see the Clanton gang half a block away. The outlaws were standing near Fry's Photography Gallery. Sheriff Behan was with them, trying to talk them into giving up their guns. Ike said he was unarmed and the others refused to listen to Behan's advice.

Ike Clanton made one threat too many. After a night of drinking, he bragged that it was time to take on the Earps. When the showdown came, Ike was not armed. He fled from the scene when the shooting started.

As the Earps moved closer Behan hurried toward them, begging them to stop. Virgil brushed the sheriff aside. At that point Behan and Billy Claiborne hid inside Fry's Gallery. The Clantons and McLaurys waited with their backs up against the small house next door.

Soon the grim-faced men were only six feet apart. The Earps had their enemies boxed in. Virgil ordered the four outlaws to lay down their guns. Billy Clanton and Frank McLaury made the mistake of cocking their pistols. In the next instant the shooting started.

Wyatt's first shot wounded Frank, who staggered into the street. Billy hurried his return shot and missed Wyatt. Morgan turned his gun on Billy, shooting him in the wrist and chest. Ike wrestled with Wyatt, but Wyatt pushed the unarmed man away. Ike scurried into Fry's Gallery. A moment later he ran out the back door and fled. Tom McLaury was yelling that he was unarmed. He tried to grab a rifle from Frank's horse, but he was not fast enough. The horse reared, giving Doc time for one shot. Deadly shotgun pellets ripped through Tom's vest. He dragged himself away, only to collapse at the corner.

Billy and Frank were still firing from where they lay. One of Billy's bullets hit Virgil in the leg. Frank got off a shot that plugged Doc in the hip. A second later Morgan put a slug below Frank's ear. Next Billy turned his fire on Morgan and hit him in the shoulder. Then he tried to stand up, but Wyatt and Morgan shot him down.

Even as Billy lay dying, he begged for more shells for his empty gun.

Although the battle lasted less than a minute, both McLaurys and Billy Clanton were dead. Virgil, Morgan, and Doc were bleeding from their wounds. As the smoke cleared Sheriff Behan came out of his hiding place. He charged the Earps and Doc Holliday with murder.

Public feeling in Tombstone was split. One side stood up for the Earps, the other backed Sheriff Behan. When

The McLaury brothers, Tom (left) and Frank (right), hated the Earps. Both brothers died in the shootout at the O.K. Corral. Tom and Frank were experienced gunslingers, but they were not quick enough that day.

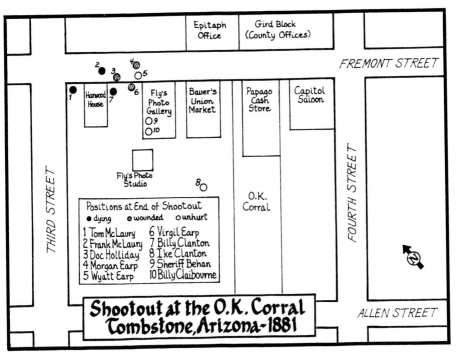

The shootout at the O.K. Corral was badly named. As this diagram shows, the shooting took place almost half a block away. The eight men were all within a few yards of each other when the first shots were fired. Less than a minute later, the shooting was over. Three men were dead and three were wounded.

the trial came it dragged on for a month. After all the testimony, Judge Wells Spicer ruled that the Earps had acted within the law. He said they had the right to defend themselves while doing their duty.

Virgil went back to his post as town marshal after his wound healed. One night, just after Christmas, he set out on patrol. From the darkness some men opened fire on him with shotguns. Wyatt heard the gunfire and ran to the scene. He found Virgil bleeding from wounds in his thigh and left arm. A doctor had to remove four

33

inches of bone from the arm. Virgil's injuries left him with a crippled arm and a bad limp.

Wyatt was sure Ike Clanton and his friends had ambushed his brother. Ike laughed at the charges when he heard them. He had sixteen men lined up to swear he had not been near Tombstone that night. Sheriff Behan said he believed Ike's alibi. Virgil was too badly hurt to take a hand in the matter. He had to resign as marshal.

The town was quiet for three months. In March Wyatt and Morgan spent a night at the theater. Afterward Morgan went to shoot some pool. Wyatt felt sleepy, but he had a hunch there might be trouble. He joined Morgan at the pool hall.

Three of Ike's men were in town that night. Pete Spence saw Wyatt and Morgan playing pool and told the others. Frank Stilwell, Spence, and Indian Charlie crept up to the back door. Suddenly the glass shattered as a six-gun blazed. The two bullets missed Wyatt, but Morgan was standing in the line of fire. One of the slugs hit him in the spine.

Some men carried Morgan to a couch. "This is the last game of pool I'll ever play," he gasped.

A witness told Wyatt he had seen the three men running away. As Wyatt watched his brother die he made a vow. The Clantons will pay in blood for shooting Morgan, he promised.

6

TOMBSTONE AND BEYOND

On the Monday after Morgan's death Wyatt put Virgil and his wife on a train. Virgil's wounds were still healing and Wyatt wanted him out of Tombstone. He then placed Morgan's body on the same train. Virgil said he would bury his brother in the Earp family plot in Colton, California.

Wyatt and Doc Holliday rode the train as far as Tucson. Word had reached them that Morgan's killers had been seen there. In their minds the debt had to be paid in blood.

That night Wyatt watched Virgil's train pull out of the Tucson station. As it gained speed the train's headlamps revealed four men hiding in the shadows. Wyatt and Doc went after them. The men split up and ran. Wyatt, shotgun in hand, cornered one of them in the dark railway yard. He was Frank Stilwell.

Stilwell did not draw his guns. Wyatt, blinded by his desire for revenge, did not seem to notice. He blasted Stilwell with the shotgun. "I let him have both barrels," he later told his lawyer. "I have no regrets. I know I got the man who killed Morg."

In Tombstone Ike Clanton swore out a warrant against Wyatt and Doc. The legal paper charged them with Stilwell's murder. At the same time Wyatt obtained a warrant of his own. It named Indian Charlie and Pete Spence as Morgan's killers.

Two posses now took to the desert around Tombstone.

The Crystal Palace was one of Tombstone's finest saloons. Miners often left a week's wages here on a Saturday night. Besides gambling and drinking, there was little else for work-weary men to do.

Sheriff Behan's posse was made up of Clanton men. Its job was to find and arrest Wyatt and Doc. Wyatt said he and his posse were going to clean out the county's outlaws. If the two posses met there was certain to be gunplay.

Wyatt and his men tracked Indian Charlie to a waterhole. Charlie tried to run for it, but Wyatt cut him down. That took care of two of Morgan's killers, he reckoned.

At this point the stories differ. Some accounts say that the two posses did have a shootout. If Wyatt's side was telling the truth at least five slugs ripped through his hat. Untouched by the bullets, Wyatt then killed Curly Bill Brocius with his shotgun. The anti-Earp accounts dispute this version. They say that Curly Bill was far from Tombstone at that time. More to the point, this side claims that the two posses never met.

For Wyatt and Doc the game was over. They had to leave Tombstone. Friends told them that Sheriff Behan planned to arrest them. Once you're in jail, they warned, you will never get out again. Wyatt and Doc did not argue. They packed up and headed north to Colorado.

Wyatt's friend Bat Masterson owned a gambling hall in Gunnison, Colorado. Bat talked to Governor Pitkin about Wyatt and Doc. Pitkin agreed that sending the pair back to Tombstone would mean certain death. When the request came to extradite Doc he turned it down. With Tombstone behind him Wyatt started a new life. He and Doc split up, although they remained good friends. Doc died in bed of his lung ailment five years later. Wyatt also left Mattie Blaylock behind. He had lived with Mattie in Tombstone but had not married her. Now he went back to the card tables. As skillful with cards as with a gun, he left Gunnison with $10,000 in his pocket.

Wyatt was still footloose. He looked for gold, but without success. Drifting on to the West Coast he turned to real estate. San Diego was booming and for two years Wyatt made money buying and selling land there. Moving north he began to buy race horses. From his farm near San Jose he raced them on both the West and East coasts.

Johnny Ringo was one of the best-known members of the Clanton gang. Wyatt may have thought he was mixed up in the shootings of Virgil and Morgan. Johnny died while Wyatt's posse was scouring the desert, looking for Morgan's killers. Some say he killed himself— but his rifle was found many yards from his body.

Wyatt's friend Bat Masterson owned gambling halls in towns like Trinidad, Colorado. These towns were full of miners with money in their pockets. Wyatt took some of that money away from them at the faro and poker tables.

Earp's name hit the headlines again in 1894. The Southern Pacific Railroad was having labor troubles. Fearful that its pay train would be held up the railroad hired Wyatt as a guard. The train's route ran from Oakland to El Paso and included many stops. With Wyatt riding in the cab of the locomotive, no one tried to stop the train. The payroll money went through safely.

Wyatt was also offered the job of U.S. Marshal of Arizona that same year. The offer surprised him because he thought he was wanted for murder there. Now he learned that the old charges had been dropped. Even so, Wyatt turned down the job. He knew that young gunmen would try to win fame by killing him. A marshal should keep the peace, not cause more deaths, he said.

Wyatt was still looking for a big strike. When gold was found in the Klondike in 1897 he headed for Alaska. He did not strike it rich, but Wyatt knew how to make money. Amid the tents of Nome he built the city's first wooden building. The Dexter Saloon was soon turning a nice profit.

For much of this time Wyatt lived with Josephine "Josie" Marcus. Wyatt had first met the actress in Tombstone. She had been Sheriff Behan's girl, but it was Wyatt who won her heart. Josie was half Wyatt's age but his match in courage. When Wyatt went into the desert to look for gold Josie went with him. Some experts say the couple never married. Josie claimed they were wed when they returned from Alaska.

At last the Earps hit it rich in the Colorado River valley. Their claim there turned into the Happy Day gold and copper mines. With the mines earning money, luck smiled on Wyatt once more. A drilling rig hit oil on his land in central California.

Wyatt settled down to a quiet life, managing his mines and oil wells. His doctor reported that the old gunslinger's body did not show a single bullet scar. One by one his parents and his brothers died. Only one sister outlived him.

Death came when Wyatt Earp was eighty years old. He died in Josie's arms on January 13, 1929. His ashes have been scattered, but his name lives on as a legend of the Old West.

At age eighty, Wyatt was still active and alert. He owned mines and oil wells, but he still liked to talk about his life in the West. One of his complaints was that no one had made a movie about his life.

7

THE LEGEND OF WYATT EARP

Wyatt Earp's fame has grown since his death. Most of the books and all of the TV shows and movies about him came after 1929. His friends said Wyatt wanted his story to be told. That was why the old marshal worked with Stuart Lake on a book about his life. Lake later published the book under the title, *Wyatt Earp: Frontier Marshal.* Although the book was more fiction than fact, the public loved it.

How much of Wyatt's fame as a lawman is based on fact? As is often the case, there are two sides to the story. His critics point out that he was a peace officer for only ten years. What kind of lawman, they add, would own saloons and gambling halls? Further, they charge him with a number of killings. In fact, Wyatt did leave Tombstone with a murder charge hanging over him.

A careful look at the record clears Wyatt of most

"EPITAPH BUILDING DAILY & WEEKLY.
CHAS. D. REPPY, EDITOR & PROPRIETOR, TOMBSTONE, ARIZONA.

The legend of Wyatt Earp was helped along by this newspaper. The Tombstone Epitaph supported the Earp brothers during their years in Tombstone. The editor sometimes printed stories about Wyatt that were more fiction than fact. Repeated many times, those stories are still being told today.

charges. In the cowtowns of the Old West a ten-year career as a lawman was a lifetime. More to the point, Wyatt brought law and order with him when he came to town. Crime rates tumbled when he patrolled the streets of Wichita and Dodge City. As for his investments, most early lawmen owned saloons and gambling halls. Wyatt seldom passed up a chance to make a profit.

The charge that Wyatt enjoyed killing is the most unfair of all. At a time when gunplay was the rule, he was not quick on the trigger. Instead of shooting rowdy cowboys he often knocked them over the head with his Buntline Special. Wyatt did not believe in peace at any price, however. When Morgan was gunned down he took a bloody revenge on the men who fired the fatal shots.

The Old West had its fair share of competent, hard-working lawmen. Wyatt Earp was more colorful and more skillful than most. Despite his failings Wyatt earned his fame fairly. If you were in danger, he was a good man to have on your side.

GLOSSARY

ambush—A surprise attack made from hiding.

bail—Money paid to a court to guarantee the return of a suspect for trial.

Buntline Special—The custom-made, long-barreled Colt revolver that writer Ned Buntline gave to Wyatt Earp.

Civil War—The war between the North and South, 1861–1865.

cord of wood—A stack of firewood that measures 4x4x8 feet.

corral—A fenced area for keeping horses or cattle.

deputy—A lawman who assists a sheriff or marshal.

dime novels—Low-cost magazines that printed popular fiction during the late 1800s.

extradite—To return a suspected criminal to another state to stand trial.

frontier—A region just being opened to settlers. Life on the western frontier was often hard and dangerous.

gunslingers—Outlaws and lawmen of the Old West who settled arguments with their pistols.

legend—A story that many people believe, but which is often untrue in whole or in part.

lynch mob—An out-of-control crowd that wants to hang someone.

Mexican War—The war between the United States and Mexico, 1846–1848.

posse—A group of citizens who join with lawmen to aid in the capture of outlaws.

typhus—A disease carried by fleas. In the 1800s, people who fell ill of typhus often died.

Union—The name given to the Northern states that fought against the South during the Civil War.

warrant—A legal paper that gives a law officer the right to arrest someone for a crime.

MORE GOOD READING ABOUT WYATT EARP

Boyer, Glenn G., ed. *I Married Wyatt Earp. The Recollections of Josephine Sarah Marcus Earp.* Tucson, AZ: University of Arizona Press, 1976.

Drago, Harry. "Tombstone—the Legend That Will Not Die," and "The Last of the Fighting Earps," in *The Legend Makers.* New York: Dodd, Mead & Company, 1975. pp. 119–139.

Lake, Stuart. *The Life and Times of Wyatt Earp.* Boston, MA: Houghton Mifflin Company, 1956.

Marks, Paula. *And Die in the West—the Story of the O.K. Corral Gunfight.* New York: William Morrow, 1989.

Martin, Douglas. *The Earps of Tombstone.* Tombstone, AZ: The Tombstone Epitaph, 1959. [A collection of original newspaper stories from the Tombstone Epitaph of 1880–1882.]

Metz, Leon Claire. "Doc Holliday and Wyatt Earp," in *The Shooters.* El Paso, TX: Mangan Books, 1976. pp. 267–291.

Trachtman, Paul and Editors of Time-Life Books. "An Epic Showdown at the O.K. Corral," in *The Gunfighters.* Alexandria, VA: Time-Life Books, 1974. pp. 15–34.

INDEX